A Child's Glacier Bay

Text by Kimberly Corral
with Hannah Corral

Photographs by Roy Corral

ᙧ

ALASKA NORTHWEST BOOKS™

Anchorage • Seattle • Portland

For our parents, and Nan, whose legacy of love is a gift we share with our children.

—Roy and Kim

We gratefully acknowledge the Roberts and Debevec families for campfires and companionship; Bonnie Kaden and Kara Berg at Glacier Bay Sea Kayaks, and Glacier Bay Lodge for logistical support; naturalists Melanie Heacox and Rosemarie Salazar for manuscript review; and superintendent Jim Brady, of Glacier Bay National Park and Preserve, for special delivery of our sleeping bags.

Library of Congress Cataloging-in-Publication Data
Corral, Kimberly, 1962–
    A Child's Glacier Bay / text by Kimberly Corral with Hannah Corral: photographs by Roy Corral
        p.   cm.
    Summary: Two young Alaskans travel with their parents on a three-week sea
kayaking journey along more than 200 miles of coastline at Glacier Bay National Park and Preserve.
    ISBN 0-88240-503-9 (hardcover)
    1. Glacier Bay National Park and Preserve (Alaska)—Description and travel—Juvenile literature. 2 Sea kayaking—Alaska—Glacier Bay National Park and Preserve—Juvenile literature. [1. Glacier Bay National Park and Preserve (alaska) 2. National parks and reserves.] I. Corral, Roy. 1946- II. Corral, Hannah. 1983- ill. Title.
F912.G5C64 1998
978.6'52—dc21   97-44666
                                                                                      CIP
                                                                                      AC

Originating Editor: Marlene Blessing
Managing Editor: Ellen Harkins Wheat
Editor: Linda Gunnarson
Designer: Constance Bollen
Map: Gray Mouse Graphics

PHOTOS. *Jacket (front):* Hannah and Ben hike by Lamplugh Glacier. *End papers:* Hannah meets Lamplugh Glacier face to face. *Page 1:* Ben slides on beached ice. *Page 2:* Hannah and Ben discover shells. *Jacket (back):* Ben plays the flute.

Alaska Northwest Books™
An imprint of Graphic Arts Center Publishing Company
P.O. Box 10306, Portland, OR 97210
800-452-3032

Printed on acid-free paper in Hong Kong.

Tidewater glaciers are rivers of ice that flow to the sea.

Below: I set up the tent at each new camp.

I press my face against the small airplane window. Below is Glacier Bay. Gigantic tongues of ice stretch out to lick the sea. The June sky is as blue as the bay where icebergs float like marshmallows.

My dad first visited Glacier Bay National Park and Preserve in 1980. Riggs Glacier was his favorite then,

A harbor seal joins her newborn pup on floating ice for safety.

〰

〰

We cook in the intertidal zone so that the rising bay will wash away all food smells.

6

and now he wants to return with our family. For three weeks we will vacation there, exploring the bay's wild coastline, where we can see about a dozen glaciers up close.

"I wonder how nature has changed the bay after all these years," my dad says. "It must look different now."

As the airplane lands at Gustavus, I remember all my dad's stories about harbor seals and their pups drifting on ice floes and humpback whales lunging to scoop small fish into their big mouths. Time after time he's told me how he woke up one morning to discover fresh bear tracks in the wet sand around his tent. And now, it's so exciting to see the park for myself.

We take a short and bumpy taxi ride to Bartlett Cove. This is park headquarters, the starting point for our trip. With heavy backpacks and duffel bags, we march along a forest trail to a beach campground for the night. The air smells salty.

My dad and I hang a rain tarp between two Sitka spruces to cover our gear—just in case. We have sleeping bags, ground pads, cameras, clothing, rain boots, tents, cooking supplies, and bear-proof food containers with tons of food. My little brother, Ben, who's almost six, even brings Frank, his toy humpback whale.

We set up camp. Something moves in the bushes around us. Then we hear *hoot-hoot-hoot, hoot-hoot, hoot-hoot.*

"What's that strange sound?" I ask my mom.

"It's a blue grouse," she says. "Let's watch for him."

Left: Black oystercatchers nest on beach rocks.
Right: Neck feathers hide a yellow air sac on this male blue grouse.

〰️

Leaves rustle behind the tent.

"Look!" Ben shouts. "He's all puffed up like a balloon!"

"Only males have that yellow air sac on their necks," my dad explains. "And there's the female."

The hen springs out of the bushes. The male chases her, his gray and black tail feathers spread out like a fan.

"I wonder what other surprises we'll have, Ben," my mom says, holding him close. "Now, let's have a kiss good night. We have an early boat to catch."

Morning comes quickly. We climb aboard the *Spirit of Adventure*, a tour boat, carrying two long kayaks and all our gear. The ship will take us upbay. Over her microphone, the park ranger announces that surf scoters, a kind of sea duck, are molting their feathers and can barely take flight from the water. She points them out. Their struggling wings sound like pages flipping in a book.

There's a loud puff ahead, so we hurry to the rail. We spot the blowhole mist —but no whale yet. We wait. Moments later, a huge whale surfaces and blows even farther away. Large tail flukes follow. How quickly the whale moves through the sea! I wonder where it's going.

〰〰

Left: Orcas are the largest member of the dolphin family.
Right: Surf scoters are diving sea ducks that usually form large flocks.

toward Lamplugh Glacier, passing one rocky wall after another. One day. Two days. Three days. It's a long way.

My mom and I paddle slowly in one kayak while my dad paddles with Ben in the other. Sea slush and ice chunks begin rushing by us on a rising tide. Ben touches a passing berg and then licks his fingers for a taste. The icy air gives me goosebumps. The glacier must be close.

Suddenly, a *split, crack, crash* thunders from the glacier. A giant block of ice hits the water and explodes into a white cloud. My heart pounds. Big, rolling swells lift our kayaks like pieces of driftwood. We're riding an ocean roller coaster at the mouth of Johns Hopkins Inlet. When the sea calms, we hurry into a cove to beach our kayaks above the high-tide line for safekeeping. Within minutes, the cove is packed with new icebergs. Until the tide changes, no one can paddle in or out.

Left: We continue our journey from Johns Hopkins Inlet. Below: Icebergs break free from McBride Glacier.

13

We read quietly but Lamplugh Glacier groans and crackles.

Our yellow tent rests on a cliff overlooking the glacier's tidewater face. Rain pours. All through the night, Lamplugh Glacier creaks and moans beside us like a blue dragon with a belly ache. I wonder if the rain causes the ice to snap and pop as it trickles down the glacier's cracks, called crevasses. That's what happens when I run water over a tray of ice cubes at home.

At last the glacier dragon belches an ice block as big as a skyscraper. It hits the water like before, but this time the tide is out and the water is shallow. The earth shakes, and the entire cove empties toward a mountain across the inlet. Moments later,

14

Music from Ben's wooden flute fills the icy air.
Right: A willow ptarmigan sits in wild lupine.

the icy bay crashes back like water swishing from side to side in a bathtub, tossing jumbled chunks of ice onto the beach below.

Next morning, the weather breaks briefly. My mom and I hike on the nearby cliffs. Ben follows. My dad stays behind to photograph a pretty patch of wildflowers called lupine. He's careful not to disturb a willow ptarmigan sitting quietly on its throne of purple petals.

Harbor seals bark on drifting icebergs below. Then tall, black fins circle around them in the water. I see one, two, three, four orcas, or killer whales.

Mom, what are those orcas doing?" I ask, looking through the binoculars.

"It looks like they're hunting harbor seals," she says. "People call orcas wolves of the sea because they hunt in packs. Maybe they know that those seals have pups."

Minutes later, the orcas have moved on to hunt somewhere else. Little round seal heads pop out of the water—safe for now.

Every day, when both tide and weather are right, we pack and paddle and explore. But today we cross the West Arm to Muir Inlet on our way to Riggs Glacier.

We wake at four in the morning to catch the outgoing tide. It's hard to leave our warm sleeping bags so early. But we're lucky because there's no wind. That makes paddling easier.

I stuff a handful of wild strawberries into my mouth as we leave. They're not ripe yet, but still tasty. In minutes, we shove our kayaks into the strong current, crunching mussel shells and

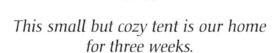

*This small but cozy tent is our home
for three weeks.*

*An early morning low tide reveals a bed of seaweed
just before we begin our day's paddle.*

~~~

brown seaweed under our rubber boots. We ride the tide
through Hugh Miller Inlet until it flushes us into the mouth of the
West Arm.

"Wow, this is really big water!" Ben says, looking at the six-
mile-wide passage.

We cruise by the last point of land, where a bald eagle sits on a
rock above the rippling tide. My mom and dad warn us that this is
a tricky passage, but I feel ready for it.

"It's safer to cross early while the sea is calm," my dad says.
"Let's get to the other side by noon before the tide changes and the

*My dad paddles hard to cross the West Arm
on the Fourth of July. Right: A bald eagle soars.*

〰〰

wind kicks in. This stretch is too big to go against both."

I turn to look at the eagle and then back again at the wide bay. Maybe the eagle is a good sign—like a guardian angel promising safe passage.

From upbay and downbay, two giant cruise ships head toward our tiny boats. They're closing in fast and looking bigger. I hope they see us. As each ship passes, we paddle straight into its large wake. We ride up one swell and then down into a deep trough as if being swallowed by the sea.

Morning becomes afternoon. The tide turns. The wind gusts. My dad and Ben fall behind. Soon the bay boils with whitecaps. Their kayak falls farther back. Sea spray chills my skin, and my arms feel like limp noodles.

My dad waves his paddle in the air to get our attention. Then he points to a raging creek tumbling off a mountain to the sea.

"He wants us to land at that boulder pile," my mom says.

We paddle toward the steep shore, but big waves crash there.

"Hannah, can you do this?" my mom asks.

"I think so."

"Okay, then," she says, on 'one-two-three,' we'll pop open our spray skirts. I'll jump out first to brace the kayak, then you'll follow. Got it?"

"Yes, captain," I say, ready to go.

On "one-two-three," we pop out and jump into the waist–deep water. Waves pound at my back. I fight to keep the kayak still, jamming my feet between slippery rocks, as my mom rushes to unload. She tosses gear onto the beach away from the rising tide. We carry the kayak next. My dad and Ben are still far away. We wait, we watch and we are soaked.

When the other kayak comes in, my mom and I hold it against the shore. My dad jumps out first; then he reaches for Ben. The wind whips, and the tide still rises. But we four are safe on land, and I'm glad.

We rest in the warm sun as the rising tide swallows the rocky beach.

"Group hug!" my dad says.

Now we can relax.

"Let's eat," he continues. "We'll paddle to the next campsite later. There are lots of great beaches around the point at Muir Inlet."

My mom boils pasta for an early dinner, while I stir chocolate pudding for dessert. We share a handful of dried apricots while my dad and Ben bathe beside the waterfall. Soon my mom and I will bathe too. With full tummies, clean bodies, and warm dry clothes, we'll be ready to go again.

For miles and days we paddle up Muir Inlet. As we travel, I notice there are fewer plants. Instead, there are more bare rocks left by the shrinking glaciers. But rocks don't stay bare for long. First, lichens and mosses take hold. Then small plants cover the rocks and begin to make soil. More and more plants and

Left top: Our journey up Muir Inlet begins.
Left bottom: Ben and I stretch our legs during a paddling break.
Above: I find these wild beach boys wearing seashells,
feathers, and black soot on their faces.

White Thunder Ridge lies across Muir Inlet,
which Muir Glacier once filled.

〜〜〜

Dryas grows near glacier edges like these at Riggs Glacier.

〰〰

bushes grow until there is a forest. My mom says this kind of change is called succession.

We paddle around one last corner to Riggs Glacier. A cloud of black-legged kittiwakes screech and dive over the spot where the glacier touches the tidewater.

"Wow, this place has changed dramatically," my dad says. "The glacier is a lot farther back now. And White Thunder Ridge is covered with green plants. It used to really be bare!"

We set up camp. My dad studies his maps. On the ridges above are small glacial ponds, called tarns, that we can explore tomorrow.

*This boreal toad is one of Ben's
most exciting discoveries.*

We wake up early the next day. The sun shines brightly in a cloudless sky.

Weather can change quickly in Glacier Bay, so we don't waste time at breakfast. Everyone pitches in. I filter water and fill all the water bottles. Ben stirs the hot cocoa. My dad boils oatmeal for breakfast while my mom prepares lunch. She makes stacks of pancakes to use as bread for the next couple of days. They taste good with peanut butter and strawberry jam, especially when they're fresh and warm. I reach for one, and bite into it. My mom smiles.

After cleanup, we hike to the tarns. The view is awesome. Riggs Glacier sits to the north, and Muir Inlet stretches out toward the south.

My mom dips her toes into the cold tarn, but I run and jump into it. My dad's camera clicks away while Ben sits in the sun.

"What's that?" Ben shouts, pointing to a ripple in the green water.

"That's a boreal toad," my dad says.

"What's a toad doing way up here by the glaciers?" I ask. We talk about how the first toad might have come over the mountains and ice. Maybe a bald eagle dropped one from its talons, or ducks carried toad eggs on their webbed feet, or some toads moved up the shoreline as the glacier moved back. One thing is certain, though—they arrived by chance.

Campfire talks are a warm way to end each day.

A new morning brings a tailwind and an outgoing tide. With such perfect conditions, it's time to paddle. We pack up and begin the last leg of our journey back toward Bartlett Cove.

At the start of our trip, my dad challenged me to build a campfire using only one match. I've done that. Now I want to build a matchless fire using embers saved under the sand.

My chance comes on one of the Beardslee Islands before going to bed. I bury the embers of the evening's campfire in a shallow layer of gravel.

In the morning, I gather dry grass and driftwood. I cut wood shavings with my pocket knife and carefully arrange them around the glowing embers. I blow gently, and the fire catches.

"Hey, Dad, I did it!" I shout. "I built a matchless fire!"

"Great, Hannah," he says, putting his arm around me.

Ben kneels in the sand and blows on his own pile of twigs and grass.

"I'm building a fire, too," he says proudly.

"I'll bet yours will be the warmest," I say.

Soon, the tide will wash away all traces of my matchless campfire.

Ben's toy whale swims in an ocean of air.

On day twenty-one, we're back at Bartlett Cove near the mouth of Glacier Bay. The sun's orange glow settles over the Fairweather Mountains. My mom and dad walk together along the beach. Ben talks to Frank, his toy whale. I sit alone on a rock left here nearly two-hundred years ago when the Grand Pacific Glacier began its retreat to create Glacier Bay.

31

The sun sets across Bartlett Cove, where the Grand Pacific Glacier reached 200 years ago.

〜〜〜

As I sit looking back on my journey, my greatest discovery happens right on this old rock. My parents say that to value something, we must know its treasures. Gulls screech. Small waves lap the shore. The warm breath of the salty sea brushes my face. The magic of this wild place is part of me now, *forever*. And, although change is constant at Glacier Bay, I hope one thing—its wildness—stays the same forever, too.

It's clear to me that wildness is the real treasure at Glacier Bay.